Anger Management for Teenagers

Urgent help for parents of teenagers who display terrible anger tendencies which are not easy to solve.

Written by
Cheryline Lawson

This book is dedicated to my loving family; especially my dear husband for always supporting me, challenging me and encouraging me in anything that I do.

"Anger, if not restrained, is frequently more hurtful to us than the injury that provokes it.".

Lucius Annaeus Seneca

All Rights Reserved © 2011 Cheryline Lawson

Disclaimer and Terms of Use: No information contained in this book should be considered as physical, health related, financial, tax, or legal advice. Your reliance upon information and content obtained by you at or through this publication is solely at your own risk. The author assumes no liability or responsibly for damage or injury to you, other persons, or property arising from any use of any product, information, idea, or instruction contained in the content provided to you through this book.

Table of Contents

Introduction	4
Anger in Society	7
A Surge of Anger	13
Minds Trapped In Anger	18
Self Esteem and Anger	25
Signs and Triggers of Anger	30
A Deeper Look Inside	36
The Teenage Years	39
The Parent's Responsibility	43
Anger Management	49
Peer Pressure - From Self or Peers	54
The Aggressive Teenager	59
Anger from a Divorce or Separation	67
The Rebellious Teen	73
Conclusion	79

Introduction

I am commonly asked questions like "Why is my teenager always angry with me?" Parents DO NOT TAKE IT PERSONALLY!

Teenagers are generally not angry with you. They are just plain angry. This anger can vary from resentment; right through to actual rage. What you are seeing is not the anger itself, but a behavior.

The emotion is the anger, but what we see is the reaction to the anger – which is the behavior.

Some teenagers withdraw and repress their anger; while others may become violent and destroy property or become physically aggressive to other people.

You, as the adult need to understand that anger from a teenager is just an emotion and not a behavior. So, the teenager doesn't have to act out their behavior in the way they do.

The anger is frequently triggered by something going on in their lives and this may be as simple as being unable to do a math problem or feeling like an outcast in a certain peer group. They may get up and walk along the corridor and punch the wall or kick a trash can, but parents - they are NOT necessarily ANGRY WITH YOU.

Often, this anger is usually not with you. It is due to a perceived inadequacy that they have. They are fearful and in this case, it is usually the fear of failure. Your teen is on an emotional roller coaster dealing with issues of identity, relationships, the future, and all their hormones are going crazy at the same time.

When you understand this, you will be able to accept that when your teen is angry, it is generally not aimed at you. Regularly, your teen is frustrated and angry with no one, but themselves.

It's really important that you, the parent; don't react to the teenager with your own anger - because this just sets up a pattern of reactive behavior from parent to teenager; going back and forth and ultimately achieving nothing positive.

This is the time that people say things that they don't mean and the situation gets out of control. In this situation, it is essential to remember that you are the adult; so stop reacting.

You need to focus more on what your teenager is feeling, and this is a way of defusing their anger. At this time, your teenage child needs some acknowledgement of their feelings. So what I want you to do when this occurs is to respond starting with the word "you."

It is very easy for us to fall into the pattern of "I can't stand it when you.. " , "I told you to...".

These are both statements in which you are responding with anger, so I want you to focus on them and their needs and commence with "you". For example, "you sound really frustrated", "you seem really distressed" or "you seem really angry today".

We all know how much better we feel when someone else acknowledges our feelings. "You're really sad today".

After you have acknowledged their feelings, it is important that you let go of the situation and at another time when the teen is not highly emotional, this is the time when you should address the issues.

For example; ask them if they had any warning signs that they were getting angry and could soon lose self control.

Often before a teen (or adult for that matter) loses control and the anger escalated into something quite ferocious, they usually find that they are clenching their fists, shaking their legs, tapping their foot, thinking weird thoughts or possibly develop sweaty palms.

Of course, each person has a different sign. If your teen acknowledges, for instance, that they get sweaty palms; just prior to an angry outburst, you can assist them in finding a less destructive activity to do when their palms sweat.

Relieving the pent up emotion, for example, with a run around the block, a swim, a shower, or even reciting a poem is the ideal action to take.

Some kind of distraction will diffuse the situation in most cases. They can now identify when their anger is escalating from the emotion into an unacceptable behavior and learn how to deal with it.

Anger in Society

Anger in society has been ongoing since the beginning of humankind's first bad decision. We look back through our history and see that anger has played a large role in society. We can also see that anger continues as the years are progressing; since more and more people are getting mad about all sorts of things.

There have been a number of reports in American where a teenager interrupted or destroyed a life due to anger. The list continues to grow to high proportions and continues to create more burdens on everyone.

We all face problems each day, but some of us more than others do. We are all subjects to anger since it is an emotion we all have. There is not one time in our lives that we all have not exploded. We may have yelled at the neighbor, a best friend, spouse, child or even our dog. We all are angry at some point in our lives.

You should never be under the impression that your child's teenage years would go by in a smooth manner. You would only be fooling yourself. You probably thought that you were mentally prepared for it. However, when you are confronted with it, the force of the impact will possibly take your breath away.

You never expected it to be so bad and needed all your mental strength and self-belief to stay calm. Most parents do have a difference of opinion when it comes to their children; even before the magical teen years, but when these differences are brought to the forefront in ways you didn't expect, it is then you experience more stress, challenge and frustration.

Let the teenager explain their side of the story and be patient in hearing it out without interrupting them or making sarcastic comments. Most of the time, all your teen child needs is for someone to hear their story and not be judgmental.

Some teens need to be encouraged to speak out and you will need to gently bring them out of their shell and give them enough confidence to express themselves.

Keep a straight face and don't try to put your teenager down by your facial expression. Don't force them into taking immediate action. It is not going to be easy for you to draw back your own actions, but you need to have as much control as you can and try to accommodate them first. This is only when they will let you in and confide in you.

The deal is learning how to cope with anger. Anger can make you or break you. In other words, your success depends on how you control your anger. You need to learn how to deal with anger when you are dealing with society as a whole; the justice system, religion, and other sources.

For example, if you were a victim to an assault and the justice system failed you; then you are mad as hell. This is ok, since you have the right to be angry. This is no different from your teenager being angry about a decision made by an administrator at school that they think is not right.

Letting that anger out, yet suppressing it to the degree that you can handle and control it, is the way to go because if you were, for example, to take action against the justice system, you would most likely end up in jail.

The same is true for the school administrator. If the teenager were to lash out angrily at a decision that the school administrator made, then that teen may find him or herself suspended from school.

If you are experiencing a problem with another individual, you have the right to contact the authorities or a teacher at your school. You have the right to protest, but not in a physical way. You have the right to contact any higher official that will work with you to find the ideal solution. You have the right to tell all the details surrounding the incidents to your parents, the authorities or your school professionals.

You do not have the right to beat someone up, attack him or her emotionally, or insult him or her verbally. You have the right to protect yourself if someone threatens your life, but you do not have the right to strike out without cause.

In certain incidents, when the other person did something to make you angry; this means that you have a right to defend yourself legally.

Being around your teen

Angry teenagers can be very difficult to be around. You may feel confused about how you feel about this because you love your child, but the reality is that sometimes you just don't like how your child behaves.

Since few parents ever talk about this even with their spouses, this suppressed feeling makes you feel guilty; even further draining your energy and setting you up for more conflict with your teen. It's a vicious cycle that leaves you wondering, "Why, oh, why can't this kid just do what he's told?"

It may help to know that even well-trained therapists have difficulty dealing with teen's anger. Of course, it is easier for them because they operate at a distance. They don't have the emotional connections or expectations that you have in your relationship with your teen.

A therapist isn't likely to feel rejected by an angry teenager who refuses to do what he or she is told. A therapist does not need to feel appreciated for his work, like a parent does; he just needs to get paid for his time spent in counseling.

The first thing you need to ask yourself when dealing with a teen's anger is what your expectations in your relationship with your teen are. Do you want your teenager to keep his room spotless, get straight A's in school and tell you how much he loves you and appreciates everything you do?

If so, this fantasy will probably never last and is just a setup for failure, disappointment and conflict between the two of you. So the first step is to examine these pie-in-the-sky expectations and bring them down to earth.

As a parent, it is your job to look to understand first and, then seek to be understood. It is not the other way around. There are certain things that you need to know. The first thing you need to know is that your child is a product of his or her hormones. Even though, this is not an excuse; it is the reality.

You still have to enforce the limits of poor behavior, but it helps to understand that your child is driven by these hormones that are surging through his or her body, which he or she is having trouble controlling and doesn't fully understand.

In other words, in many ways, your child is not in the driver's seat, so when he cuts you off, try not to take it personally. While this doesn't mean you excuse his behavior, it means you learn how to respond to it, cope with it, and rather not react to it.

Your teen is caught in an unfamiliar place; between being a child and being an adult. There is so much pressure here and it is like nothing you can imagine. Or is that you know it from the experience of being a teenager yourself in the past, but you choose not to relate to it now.

Even though, you've been there and done that, you were not forced to grow up in such a complicated and difficult world with so many distractions and choices to make. The pressure from all this can be overpowering and can make your child feel like it's just better and less perplexing not to care.

Although there will be plenty of interactions with your angry child that leave you feeling like you don't like your teen, you do love him and it's your job to do what is best for him. Do this not by being a "sage on the stage," but by being a "guide on the side," which is a skill that you can adapt to.

When you're not preaching from your pulpit, but allowing your teenager to discover how the world works with your delicate guidance, you are less liable to take the behavior personally.

This is especially so when you understand that while you may not like the improper behavior and feel annoyed with the apparent inability to learn; deep down you still love your teen child more than anything else.

For parents who have difficulty taking care of tough situations with their children (and believe me, we all do), there are outside resources that can help.

Be empathic toward your child. Let the child know that you, too, were once a teenager and can identify with some of the things he or she is going through. Don't act as if you know it all. A teenager likes to be validated and listened to. They don't want to feel as you think that 'a child should be seen and not heard.'

A teenager wants to have the reassurance that he or she can voice an opinion without being ridiculed and chastised by you, the parent. They want some leg room, even though, they know that you have the 'last say.'

While a therapist can help your child learn to deal with his anger, a better tact is to learn how to do this yourself. By doing so, you will increase your skill as a parent, gain your child's respect and ultimately, create a closer relationship with your child.

A Surge of Anger

We walk through life searching for ways to understand how anger interrupts so many lives, including our own. Some people forget about when they were once teenagers.

With that deliberate lack of memory and a change in societal issues, most parents really don't understand what their children are going through. Some don't take the steps necessary to really understand what it is like to be in their children's shoes in this current environment and most fail to listen to their children.

Again, most times, when teens get to the point of anger is when they feel that they are not being heard. There could be other reasons to their anger, but in most cases, it is because they think that society does not understand them and neither does their parents.

We should talk with them about their anger and ask what the reasons for their angry are. You need to get to the bottom of the problem because nine times out of ten, the issue started longer than you could imagine, but got to a point where it was more difficult for your teen to deal with it. So your teenage child lashes out; not knowing what else to do.

There may be minor inconveniences or there may be a situation where the teen feels cheated, hurt or absolutely frustrated. There are different ways your teenager can react to these situations and a wise parent can provide guidance and instructions on how to be aware of the different kinds of reactions which might be justified.

Anger may well be justified in a situation where the teen has been hurt. As adults, we do get angry too when the situation warrants it. So after you have listened to what your child has to explain about their anger, then you will provide guidance in how to resolve the problem now or the next time it happens.

Some parents seem to be living on a different planet. Well, that is what your teenage child thinks anyway. You may have thought that your teen was this peaceful being, but when you started receiving reports of violent behavior from school administration and of bullying, you thought the school was blowing it out of proportion.

However, when your child punches a classmate in the nose; resulting with blood spewing all over the place, you, then knew that you can no longer ignore it or sweep it under the rug. It is time for you as a parent to look at what is causing this and finding the solutions of your teen's anger.

The easiest way to drive your teenager further away will be to react angrily, shout and abuse them. Such a reaction would only further aggravate the situation. So what do you as a parent do now?

Do you just wish that all this disappears on its own or do you try to console your child or listen more attentively? Most teenagers are confused souls seeking a direction in life.

We can see through the history that anger has been a major problem in the world. We know that we have a diverse world, which includes different classes, genders, race, ethnicity, and so forth. We know that society has its own rules, the law has its rules, and the religious leaders have their rules.

We also know that there are different countries that have their own beliefs; having a different understanding than some do in other countries. This means that we are living in a diverse system and that there needs to be understanding in order to reduce the number of anger problems around the world.

Anger is an emotion that all of us share. When anger gets the best of us, then it is time to find anger management solutions to deal with the stress. The many people that are angry find it difficult at times to adhere to the different techniques offered since all of us differ in our own way. As adults, we have angry bouts from time to time, so why can't we learn to identify with our own children when they get angry?

Some of us can go for a walk and cool down, while others may walk and find it difficult to find relief. This is because the person is focusing on his or her madness and refuses to let go. When this occurs, it might be best to find another strategy that works for you.

You might find a soft cushion and beat it until your frustrations are exhausted. You might even try writing down your feelings on paper and reviewing the list once your anger is vented on paper.

Whatever works for you may not work for your teenage child, but you can work with your teenager to find what works best for him or her. Beating a pillow or cushion might sound funny or crazy to some, I guess, but you would be surprised that it works for some.

Feeling as if you have won will generally enhance your teenager's mood. If you find the pillow beating absurd or difficult, you may want to take a blank paper and draw ugly faces. You can draw your emotions and feelings on a piece of paper and this often works for some to relieve the anger and the stress.

After your teenager finds the technique that works best for him, then it is time to learn how to deal with anger by finding the triggers and learning strategies to avoid them. Anger management classes teach us to control our anger, by looking at the triggers, emotions, and person as a whole. For example, if you were to get angry because someone ate the last cookie you had, then you know you have a problem with selfishness.

A cookie is no reason to explode and vent your anger on another person. Material is irrelevant compared to hurting another individual.

When you cuss, argue, fight or threaten someone because of your anger, you are not only harming yourself; since anger harms your body, you are hurting the other person as well.

Dancing and other extracurricular activities such as basketball is also great for relieving tension, stress, anxiety, and depression. If your teenagers have any of these or other skills, you should encourage them to put them to good use, since this can help to manage the anger.

Once your teenager steps to the beat of the music, they should put their hearts into it by listening to the sounds and voices of the musicians.

Absorbing your mind into music has proven effective for relieving emotional stress. Getting lost in a world of illusion can benefit the mind when the mind has taking all it can take. The problem is deeper than the cookie; therefore your teen can learn from each strategy what really makes him or her mad.

We all have problems we face each day, and some of us have more than others do. Therefore, facing reality in full light is great for controlling anger. When you realize that you are not being focused on and attacked because of who you are; you will then realize that problems are solvable. For example, even you, as an adult going through financial problems, should realize that you can research and learn how to find a resolve for this problem.

Teach your teenager how to do this. For every problem, there is a positive and negative reaction and solution. Teach your teenager how to gravitate towards the positive reaction and solution.

Once your teenager gets positive insight, it will lead him or her to take the steps to relieving the stress and anger. If the problem is family, your teen might look at both sides to see where he or she can make things better.

If someone else is the problem, your teen might ask this person in a calm voice to better him or her selves, since they are creating a problem. A surge of anger is great if you can control it and not let it get out of control at any time!

Minds trapped in anger

When we have a flamboyant personality type, then we are prone to anger outbursts. A person with flamboyant thoughts may believe that he or she is already focused on compared to everyone else when he or she does not get his or her way. People with these types of attitudes will say things like, "that was a lousy idea, since those people are stupid anyway."

A person of this nature may believe that other people would have behaved the way that they did in a similar situation. There are many traits to being pompous that are disturbing and when a person has a disturbed mind, he or she is prone to anger. This type of person will have a difficult time dealing with stressors and stress and will often act out on emotions when they feel threatened.

This means they are prone to assaulting others; showing off their intellect, cursing at the problem, attacking another person's mental status, and even acting out violently when they are mad. This type takes us to a whole new level of understanding anger, since mental illness is often the underlying emotions. A person of this magnitude of anger is known as a narcissistic personality type.

Paranoid schizophrenias, histrionic personality types and a few others have a ostentatious personality underlying the diagnosis. When we see that a person is angry due to mental illness, then anger management may or may not work. Most histrionic personality types are firm in their way of thinking, therefore more extensive therapy is needed to deal with this type.

If you experienced anger outbursts, you realize that you feel remorse after the interruption takes place. On the other hand, if you have a histrionic or paranoid personality, remorse is not in the picture. A person has to have a sense of remorse to become subject to recovery in anger management.

Although the psychotherapist may find a resolve, it will be minimal. Unfortunately, in some cases of this type of anger, there is no resolve and the patient may eventually destroy another person's life. Uncontrolled anger includes, striking, hitting, punching, assaulting mentally, verbally assault, and even murder.

Now we are looking at a serious problem, since anyone is at risk of being subjected to these types of personality. A more common form of anger is a mild name calling, such as, "you were acting like a jerk. Alternatively, damn why did you do that?"

Some of us might even say why you centered me out as a target to anger. The person will raise the voice assertively, and often walk away when the person does not reply as he or she intended. There are forms of anger that can be dealt with and some are rooted from jealousy. Some are more severe when it can result in traumatic situations like murder.

The problem is dealing with it so that it does not get the best of you. For example, if you are married and suspect that your spouse is having an affair you might confront this person rather than being accusatory. Find out the details before you blow up and cause a commotion. If the person is cheating, then you have two options.

You can forgive the person's infidelity and move on or you can hire a lawyer to get a divorce or find a more suitable, trusting mate to get married to. Each person should choose what works best in their situation, but instead of sending up your 'blood pressure,' because of what someone else does, is not going to resolve the situation.

I would choose to try to move on or if I couldn't, I would then try to speak calmly to the other person; letting them know how badly they had hurt you and discuss how to fix it.

See the reasoning behind this? Of course, it is going to hurt, but in the end, you would either have made a good or bad choice, but not one that included anger. Forgiveness frees your spirit. It discards any signs of anger. You will be a better person for it.

If you decide to stay with the person, remember you forgave so do not bring up failures when another problem occurs. Failure is success flipped over and if you review failure in a positive light, your problems will be less as you move forward in life.

Many teenagers go through similar things when it comes to relationships as adults do; so the same is true for them too. If someone has a pompous personality, they will need help, since things are going to be difficult for them to accept. They should not let failure control their anger before it controls their life.

Parents can help their teenagers realize this before it happens. Nothing is cut in stone. Things can happen in life that will cause you or others to mess up. This does not mean that you have to stay angry. You can choose to forgive and move on or be asked to be forgiven and move on. Teenagers are going to have to deal with these and other situations in life.

During their school years, it is vital that they understand that society is waiting to challenge how they will handle themselves. There are so many situations that they will encounter and some of these situations will warrant their being able to stay cool, calm and collective.

They need to learn social skills from home first and then how to deal with their teachers, friends and classmates. Without social skills, anger is more prone to affect them in an adverse manner.

Your teenager needs to know that when he or she is mad, it consumes so much more energy and they spend too much time on negative forces that may or may not glean the results that will help them to grow. Anger is an emotion that we all have and when we use anger to our advantage, it often takes us further.

Anger that strikes, hits, punches, curses, assaults, and displays negative emotions can become the cause of more problems. Dealing with emotions and anger is never easy when we have probable cause to become angry. When others hurt our feelings, attack our intellect, and take advantage of us, it can upset anyone.

Instead of resolving their problems, teenagers can add more problems to everyone's life. When you expose uncontrolled anger, you are not only hurting yourself, but you are hurting other people.

Anger is increasingly causing more problems for society and that is why so many young adults end up in jail. Since we are dealing with terrorist, serial murders, child and spouse abuse and other types of violence, we know that the world is heading for disaster, unless someone comes up with the master plan to deal with all the anger surfacing the earth.

If we are going to get ahead in life, we have to find a way to deal with anger on all levels. Some of us act out violently while others find a more suitable way to deal with problems. If we use anger positively, then we are sure to have a much more productive life. For example, you can be angry about an issue, that if resolved can produce a positive outcome and that is why we have so many activists in our society – for change.

In a way, we all rely on each other; whether it is directly or indirectly. Anger rules the world at this point since we are all touched by the violence that plagues our system. It starts in the home, then in our schools and seeps out in the world.

However, if we all take the first step in dealing with our emotions and anger, then our lives will benefit society at large. Your teenagers need to know these things and who better to tell them, but you, the parent.

Anger is either negative or positive. When we are angry, we often walk away from a problem or else handle it by screaming at the source. Anger is an emotion that either controls us or helps us to succeed in life.

If we have negative thoughts most likely when a threat hits our emotion, we will explode. Some of us abuse others by, hitting, slapping, verbally assaulting, mentally abusing, or punching walls or other obstacles to vent our anger.

We can break this down and see that nothing, but harm comes from these actions. If your teenager is hitting or slapping another person, he or she will end up in jail and that person may end up in the hospital. Once a person is hit, even if they do not go to the hospital, the emotional scar will remain for years. Hitting does not solve any problems. It only worsens it.

Likewise, if your teenager is punching walls, glass, or other things, it could cause harm to them. If they are verbally or mentally abusing another individual, they are scaring him or her for life. It makes no sense to behave negatively or harmfully when a person is angered. The best solution is learning to deal with these emotions, since most times, emotions will play tricks on someone's mind.

Your teenager may have misunderstood the person that they felt made them angry and made them feel that they had to act out on an emotion that makes them look foolish in the situation. This is only humiliation of self and leads nowhere. If your teen has a hard time comprehending what you are saying, then they will do the same to others outside of the home.

They should know that it is best to slow down and ask the person to explain. This often will clear things up and your teenager may see that the person was not threatening their emotions in anyway. If your teen feels that no one listens to them, then they might ask themselves, if it is just a part of their imagination, or is it true that no one hears?

Your teenager needs to understand that he or she cannot blame others for their behavior or action. When a person behaves in a derogatory way, then it affects other people.

When a person becomes a victim of an angry person, they often learn the same behaviors and act accordingly to how they were being treated.

This means that we have more problems in society, and no one wins. Life is too short and filled with too many problems already to create more problems.

If your teenager cannot find a way to control their anger, it might be best to find someone that they trust to help them control and handle their emotions in a positive way.

Their young lives are riding on this! Teenagers don't realize that they have a bright future ahead of them that uncontrolled anger can destroy. It is up to parents to relay this message; not in a condescending way, but in a loving way.

Self Esteem and Anger

How does self-esteem play a part in emotions and anger? When a person (including your teenager) has low self-esteem, they are subject to anger, since their emotions are off balanced. When a person feels good about themselves, they often have self-control, which makes their life easier.

They are capable of socializing without running into problems of how to articulate and explain themselves without displaying anger. Everyone has problems, but when we have self-control, other people will see it from afar.

When others see a confident person, they are willing to associate with the person and may even wonder what the person does to have such a wonderful attitude. On the other hand, when a person has self-esteem issues, they are often looked down upon since their behavior is evidence of their problem.

Why does your teenager have self-esteem problems? Self-esteem is respect for oneself, and confidence within. When we feel in control of ourselves, we often know how to avoid problems efficiently. Usually when a person has low self-esteem, they often connect with others that have aggressive mental issues, low self-image, and more problems than the average person has to deal with.

When a person feels bad about their self-worth, they will often get involved in risky activities or take harmful substances such as drugs or alcohol that only increase anger. We are all different in our own way. Some of us are abused, some heavy, some skinny, some beautiful and some are not.

Adults can look at this in many different ways, rather than dwelling on what we cannot change. However, your teenager may not see it that way. For your teen, keeping up appearances in school is more important to them than anything else. They aspire to be part of the crowd – to fit in.

Your teenager does not realize that many of the beautiful people in the world prove ugly inside since their personalities illustrate unruly behaviors or attitudes.

Therefore, is your suffering from low self-esteem? If your teen is, then he or she might want to boost that image, since many people like to be around people who are innately good and confident.

If your teenager sees how self-esteem makes or break a person, your teen will know that this may be an instigator to their anger. We all deal with anger differently. When we deal with anger in a positive way and find a good outcome, then we will know that we have to control it.

On the other hand, if we are forcing our emotions to believe we are less than others are, then we do not have control, but rather we have anger under the surface and at any time, and we are ready to explode.

Let's review your teen's self-esteem:

How does your teen feel inside most days?

Does your teen think that he or she is a good person and feel that their life is in control?

Does your teen spend hours in the closet trying to find an outfit that will enhance their looks?

Does your teen spend hours in the mirror studying their features; wondering what they can change about their appearance?

These are a few of the signs that tell us what type of self-esteem your teen has. Most likely, your teen may have endured some bad experience in the past that contributed to their self-image; therefore he or she needs to examine their inner self and inner child to find out what occurred that made them feel the way they do.

Your teen may be angry because of how people have treated them in the past and probably feel self conscious about it. Someone else let your teen down, which threatened their emotions and this is where the anger may lie. If your teen has anger issues, get help for them. There is nothing wrong with doing so!

Frequently when a person is angry, the person feels unsure of his or herself. If your teenager does not feel secure, then they will feel unsure of themselves. When they are challenged, the first line of defense will be anger.

If they are fearful and have doubts about trusting others, then they are open to harm by others. This means they are susceptible to being taken advantage of. This will only put their guard up and make them always on the defense when dealing with others. They will always think the worst about what others mean when they speak to them. They will blow simple things out of proportion, which will enforce angry outbursts.

If your teenager feels vulnerable, then this is only opening up doubts and a lack of self esteem. When a person's self image has been tarnished, then anger is always under the surface and when emotions feel threatened, your teen is most likely to explode.

When a person loses the feeling of control, then this person will most likely strike when another person threatens his or her emotions. Consequently, we see that feeling secure plays a role in anger, as well as control.

Anger management is a sort of psychotherapy that teaches us to control our anger, which means we are in control of our emotions and life. Anger management also teaches us how to cope with problems; how to keep away from or handle our triggers, and how to provide a measurable amount of security.

For example, if your teen grew up in a home, where no one sat at the table and ate dinner together or alternatively, if the family had a breakdown in communication; your teenager will be the kind of person that never was taught to be sociable effective and won't be able to handle confrontations. This means that your teenager has to be in situations where they know how to interact with others without losing control of their anger

Emotions run deep and we all have scars from our past. We could still live in a prominent home, but somewhere during our life, we are going to experience problems. It does not matter what kind of home structure a teenager lives in, anger can happen to both the rich, middle income and the poor. Problems and issues are all around us; not necessarily in the home.

It is how we teach our teenagers to deal with those problems is what will give them the control and security that they need to function properly in life.

There is no escaping life's many problems. Our teenagers need to learn how to manage the stressors that knock on their doors every day.

You may wonder if a teenager has stress and how could they? Yes, they do. Too much homework can be a stress factor for a teenager.

Preparing for college, having a boyfriend, and building relationships are ways that your teenager can be stressed out. A teenager can get angry over any of these issues at any time; especially if they are not getting as much support from the parents.

Anger management is the solution if your teenager cannot control or deal with anger; no matter how small. You may also want to consult with an expert for teen evaluation.

Signs and Triggers of Anger

"Why am I so angry all the time?" We have all asked this question at some point in our lifetime. The best way to answer is to reach deep in your own past and search for the answers.

This might be very difficult for a teenager. Having full control of their life is virtually challenging, since teenagers have to be accountable to their parents and others for their actions.

This causes anger for some, since they may have endured a life with a controlling person, or parent. Teenagers all have rules to follow and this often discourages them when they feel that certain rules are ridiculous.

Teens may live with their family and at times, someone gets on their last nerves. They may have part time jobs and feel that the job is just not happening, and wish they had a better opportunity of making more money. They may go to school and someone is bullying them, or intimidating them emotionally.

There are many reasons a teenager can get angry and some of the above mentioned examples are justifiable, but still need to be controlled. What matters most is how they learn to cope with their anger. Either, your teenager can take the path to destruction or can take the road to walking away.

Either way, your teenager will feel some kind of anger and the road to controlling the anger has many bumpy areas. No one has a perfect life. Teenagers are still learning how to cope with this new adult world and so it is the parent's duty to inform and educate their teens on the realities of life.

What are the signs of anger? Since everyone is different it can be impossible to define; however since all anger is the same, we can sum it up. Angry persons will assault others, whether it is verbally or physically.

An angry person will slap, hit, punch, threaten, shove, or kick others when their anger arises. They are often aggressive, sarcastic, nagging, and will often complain about everything. They are malicious toward others, which includes spreading rumors, retaliating, or defiantly striking out against another.

Persons with anger problems often display anti-social behaviors, including denial and inability to relate to others. Angry persons often act out in hate and will go out of their way to hurt others in the process.

They often have negative thinking patterns and these patterns are displayed toward others. When a person is angry, they often tell others that they are stupid.

Alternatively, 'you are ugly and no one wants you,' are some things that an angry person would think and say. This is belittling the other person and the angry person often finds relief in it; sometimes even enjoyment. When a person has difficulty dealing with his or her anger they will often vent their lack the ability to trust others.

They are often suspicious, whining, judgmental, and often jealous of others. They will act out disruptively, and retort to disobliging reactions. A person with anger issues will often try to undermine anyone around them. These types of people are no fun to be around and they do need help.

Angry people, in fact, display anti-social behaviors, and often communicate erupting thinking patterns. There are different things that can trigger anger.

Triggers are what interrupt the emotions and causes us to become angry. When we learn our triggers, we are taking a step in the right direction to control our emotions.

First, we need to weed through the roots of anger to determine the problem. If you have obsessive anger and outbursts, you might want to see an expert for help to eliminate the roots of your anger. You will then need to attend anger management classes.

Obviously, you have no control over your emotions; therefore, you will need to learn techniques that help you to cope better with your fears, frustrations, anxiety, depression and emotions. This will help you to move ahead in life and gain control of your anger.

You might want to ask yourself what you are afraid of or what are the triggers of your anger? You might review the thoughts carefully to see if you anger is understandable. Are you afraid to speak up and protect your rights? Is there something in your past that leads you to worry obsessively and initiate your anger?

Maybe you were a victim of some incident in your past or you witnessed something that disturbed your subconscious and you rambled through life without dealing with it.

Regardless, you are affected somehow and your emotions are not cooperating with your thoughts. Some of us fret over things that are out of our control and then let it get the better of us.

For example, many of us worry about adapting to certain situations or being respected by others, which is not in our hands to worry about? We cannot control how others treat us and teenagers need to learn this.

We are responsible for our own emotions and actions, but yet fail to take charge of them; allowing them to rule our lives.

We might even find a source in the past that invoked our emotions and promoted an undeveloped mind. When you find your triggers and review your problems, you are taking charge of your anger and your life will prove fruitful for your efforts.

Triggers are objects, words, pictures, sound, taste, smell and when a person is triggered to anger; they often react either positively or negatively to the source. There will always be things that trigger our anger, but it is how we react to these triggers that will make or break us.

Anger management will teach teenagers different skills for controlling their emotions. So this would be the ideal solution in a perfect world.

However, there are other things that need to be done and parents play a key role in helping their teenage child to take responsibility for their actions.

Reasoning with the emotions to avoid anger can prove productive over time. Emotions need to be fed positively just as our body needs food to survive.

When we are facing the reality of our uncontrolled emotions, then we are enforcing our ability to manage our anger. For example, if you are reasoning that the current situation cannot be resolved, then you are setting your emotions up to explode when a trigger is hit.

How we perceive each problem makes a difference to the emotions. If we are thinking negatively, then we will likely endure the outcome when we explode. On the other hand, if we feed our emotions with positive thinking, then our life is heading down in the right direction. This is where education comes into play.

When we erupt in anger, we are only throwing fuel on an existing fire. Most emotional problems stem from faulty beliefs and teaching; therefore parents need to provide the required education and information, which will play a large role in their teenage child's life. In addition, learning from many sources can teach your child how to behave in life.

We all add problems to our life by stressing over things that are not in our control. When we learn to take it one day at a time or appreciate what we have, we are taking the steps to controlling our emotions and life.

Reasoning with the emotions to avoid anger is simply. If you are thinking, negative thoughts flip it around and start thinking positively. What lessons can you glean from your angry outburst?

When you are reviewing a problem, take a look at both sides to see where you fit in the picture. If you are adhering to behaviors that instigate the problem, find a way to resolve by taking a positive approach and deal with your anger.

Walking away from situations that cause anger does not mean that you are weak or a sissy as many high school teens will tell you. It means you are a strong. It takes a stronger person to walk away from a volatile situation. It takes a weak person to succumb to it.

Good and bad comes to us all, but the power is put in our hands in dealing with the emotions and reasoning associated with the source of the problem.

A Deeper Look Inside

Negative thinking channels the attitude of a teenager into the incorrect direction and frequently raises an individual's chance of going off when anger builds up.

Teenagers who refuse to be positive in life are generally shallow. If you think that your teenager is a hopeless case, then they will always have issues added to their everyday life. Your teenager can sense when you are negative towards them.

Being an "if" individual, will likewise set your teenager up for failure. Postulating "what if this occurs", or "what if that," may lead to irrational fear.

You need to encourage your teenage child to keep his or her mind in the correct place to see to it that they don't amass any unnecessary issues.

Motivate your teen to pay attention to matters that they are able to alter and leave the matters that they can't alter alone. Don't let them waste their time questioning and worrying about something that they know they have no effect on.

There's no need to fret about the things that happen in the past. Teenagers need to keep their thoughts unclouded and they'll be less likely to build up fear.

A few individuals set themselves up for blasts of anger by questioning something that occurred weeks ago. It is best for teens to let themselves be free from the pressure of past instances as they can't undo anything that's already been done.

They ought to learn to value what they do have command over, instead of stressing about the situations. If your teen has trouble arriving at decisions, then you should help them by providing instances of your experiences.

We all have issues making the correct decisions in life, and that doesn't mean that the world has to topple over or end.

What it means is that your teens need to learn how to be decisive in settling certain issues before they get out of control.

Here are some things you can do to help your teenager. Let your teen learn how to:

- Assess the issue cautiously
- Survey their choices for resolving the issue
- Access the resources to deal with the issue
- Find ways to solve the issue
- Come to a absolute decision
- Take steps to treat the problem right away

Putting matters off only makes things worse. Arriving at a good decision will provide a better outcome. Anger may be damaging or positive.

The emotion of anger may either control us or drive us to succeed in life. If a person's mind is filled up with negative thoughts, then they will most likely burst out in anger when something threatens the emotions.

Many times emotions will drive your teen to an irrational solution. Many times your teenaged child might get angry because they sense that somebody made them look foolish in the situation.

This is only self abasement and it's a blind way to look at things. Occasionally, your teenager may have issues understanding what somebody is saying.

The best thing to do is to step back and ask for an explanation from the individual. This often sheds a light on the state of affairs and your teen might be surprised to discover that the individual wasn't trying to endanger their emotions in any way.

Many persons feel threatened by individuals that don't listen to them when they're talking. Your teenager might be just over thinking it.

If a teenager feels violated by someone, it is best to let the person know in a calm manner.

Flaring up will only add fire to the fury. It is more likely that the person will listen to the other side of the story if it is delivered in a calm manner.

Uncontrollable anger from a teen indicates how immature and antisocial that child is.

If your teen cannot find a way to check their anger, they should find somebody that they can trust to help them to control the overflowing emotions.

Somebody else might be able to talk your teenager out of their angry behavior.

The Teenager Years

The teenage years are the most difficult time in any person's life as it is then that being positive in situations can be really challenging. Teenagers are more prone to anger.

Society, too, presents teenagers with lots of situations which anger them. Sometimes, teens have to endure a lot of jealousy and competition and this is what causes anger in most teenagers.

A lot of teenagers are not compassionate and they aggressively fight to stay on top of things; therefore, wasting the best part of their developing years - fighting with each another.

The daily challenges and various obstacles that they have to face in their daily lives make them grow up much faster than they need to. While some teenagers are able to face challenges; others just cannot do so and instead feel that they have to always be defending themselves.

It is only when they face confrontations that teenagers become angry to the extent that they can sometimes turn violent, and in some cases, this can even lead to deaths.

Teenagers normally find it very hard to listen to good counsel, so any anger management programs may not be favorable at first.

It is important that parents choose a specific and acceptable anger management program that is designed for that particular teenager.

It is really a challenging task to convince a teenager that he or she has behavioral problems. The best way is to make them understand why it is important for them to change their attitude.

Anger, when not controlled, can actually ruin a teenager's life. Teenagers, when they are consumed with anger, will normally begin to yell or scream at others by saying hurtful things that are not meant to be said.

They will even exhibit violent behavior like punching walls, pushing other people around and at times can even resort to hurting themselves.

Though, it may be difficult to convince teenagers that anger is a bad emotion it is still important to do so. Teenagers can become successful if they learn anger management techniques and where they learn how to deal with their emotions in a positive way.

This makes life much easier and enjoyable for them. A positive change happens when they learn how to control anger.

Teenagers should be educated on self awareness, where they learn the reasons that cause anger in them.

They should be taught self control where they are asked to stop and think about repercussions associated with their anger. Once they realize what the reactions would be to their behavior; they should then be taught to make choices.

This will help achieve effective results from their right choices. Teenagers are taught to act on their feelings so that they can learn all about anger management.

Once they learn the technique, regular reviews would be necessary so that they successfully implement these techniques in their lives.

They can be educated on how to use the plan in situations that make them irritated so that they can overcome the irritation successfully. This will help them to tackle all other similar situations with a positive attitude.

Most teenagers have their own opinions about what they like or dislike. Activities like exercises, music, and keeping a journal are all effective ways for anger management in teenagers.

Only when the teenager is able to accept responsibility for his or her bad behavior can they achieve success in anger management.

It is not a cut and dry situation because every teen is different. However, helping them concentrate on activities that appeal to them will help them effectively manage their anger. They can be taught to concentrate on these activities when they feel threatened by negative emotions like anger.

It is not easy to help a teenager to learn the technique of anger management but it will surely be worth their while when they turn out to be successful adults much later in life.

When you are , you don't understand the difference between a great way to cope with anger and a bad way. It is not until you are much older that you begin to determine the difference.

When your teen sees somebody, like you, the parent, cope with a situation with poise and integrity, your teen should try and integrate that into your life-style.

Therefore, you are the first example for your teenaged child. The next time something like this arises your child will know how to handle the situation in a respectful way.

This might take some time and work on their part, but they will be taking the measures necessary to recover from their anger issues.

It's really hard to go through life without being angry at something or somebody at one time or some other. The mystery is learning to cope with the anger and discovering how to effectively declare the anger without inducing harm.

For instance, if you teenager is dealing with a person that's quite self-opinionated in a matter, the teen might take offense to it. The most beneficial thing to do is change the subject or to kill them with kindness.

Altering the topic, when it is apparent that anger is the next step, will save time and energy in the long run. Your teen should probably try and talk something nice about the individual or add something nice about the matter.

It's hard to persist in a downward spiral of anger while somebody is being kind and courteous; all they can do is pause and wonder about you and what you are saying. Perhaps they even wonder if they are wrong about the matter completely.

The Parent's Responsibility

Many parents today are asking this question: "Where is my teenage child's anger coming from and why is this anger so explosive?" Teenagers, like adults, do experience pressure, anxiety and stress each day.

The stubborn and argumentative teen is fighting for freedom and less control from the parents. An angry teen battles with difficulties on a daily basis and is trying to make sense of all this emotional issues, such as:

- Visible changes in their bodies
- Trying to establish an identity
- Dealing with friends
- Positive and negative peer pressure
- The demands of school
- Separation or divorce of parents
- Being accused of something they didn't do
- Feeling that they are being treated unfairly
- Not getting a chance to voice their opinion
- A chronic illness or death of a loved one
- Taking on too many activities
- The high expectations from their parents
- Abuse of drugs or alcohol

It is no surprise that teenagers might become quite overloaded with stress. Teenagers don't have the same coping skills as adults do, and getting angry is the only way that they know how to avoid feelings of sadness, hurt and fear.

When your daughter or son tells you to get the 'F$#,' out of his or her life, this is something that you cannot forget. You remember it for the rest of your life. Why? Well, it hurts a parent to hear a child being this disrespectful.

A friend of mine told me this story about her teenage daughter:

"I remember a few years ago, I was at home cleaning up. I was supposed to be relaxing at the time, but my oldest teenage daughter had neglected cleaning her room again.

This is something that she is expected to do at least once a week. After reminding her for the 100th time that month that her room was in a mess, I had refused to clean her room myself. I angrily grabbed the vacuum and begun to clean the carpet in her room.

As frustration built with every push of the vacuum, I began to scheme her punishment. It would have to be a solid one. It would be the punishment of all punishments. I will fix her this time. I will show her the boss really is around my house. I was livid.

With sweat pouring from every pore of my body, I noticed her being dropped off by her girlfriends.

Apparently, they had all gone to a movie and then to the mall shopping. They were all laughing and having a ball. On the scale of 1 to

10; 10 being angry as hell, I was up to 8.5. I angrily flung the door open and stepped towards her to give her a taste of my angry tongue. She said to me again, "Mommy, will you get the F out of my life right now."

My jaw dropped and at that moment, I literally felt physically paralyzed. I could not move. I was so hurt by those words. It was like she had cut me with a butcher knife.

I absolutely didn't know how to react. So I just grabbed my car keys and raced off in my car. I drove around for hours feeling guilty, rejected, angry, and disappointed, but most of all, I felt resentment."

IS this how your teenager makes you react? Is it a good way to deal with it? Most experts will tell you that it is not. My friend felt, "Is this the gratitude I receive after raising this girl for the past sixteen years? How dare she talk to her mother like that?

Looking back, I know that at that time, I was not emotionally capable of handling teen anger management.

I wanted to have someone understand what I was going through. My daughter had no rights, I thought. I wanted everyone to take my side. I was the parent, wasn't I?

I should be the one who was right, and she was wrong. However, what I should have wanted was to be able to learn more about anger management for teenagers, so that the next time an explosive situation took place, I would be able to remain calm."

Since then, my friend and her daughter have healed and mended their relationship and their wounds caused by a misunderstanding, miscommunication and ultimately anger.

However, one thing is sure that they both realize that they were just at different places in their lives. They both knew that they loved each other. Cleaning her room was not a priority for my friend's daughter. She wanted to fit in with her friends, no matter what the cost.

My friend confessed that:

"I have learned to let go of my controlling when I'm dealing with my teenager." Like most parents, my friend realized that teens are bombarded every day with peer pressure, so their volatile emotions are products of their surroundings.

As parents, we have to learn our teen's language, but more significantly, we have to know what battles to fight, and what battles to walk away from.

Now that she has learned to assess her own feelings and emotions before she opens her mouth, she has learned to walk away from most heated arguments before they start.

Her daughter still has emotional roller coasters; after all she is a teen. However, my friend has equipped herself with emotional armor and techniques that will diffuse a lot of stress.

She learned to give her daughter different options instead of just telling her what to do. She would have her choose if she wanted to wash the dishes instead of washing the clothes, for example. Her daughter had no choice when it came to her room and both of them already established this.

My friend went on to say:

"It is her room and she needs to keep it clean. These are the things that have made our relationship a lot better. There are still some fights, but I know how to handle them much differently than before.

She seems much happier, and although I would like her to worship her mother like she did when she was 2 years old, I know this is not practical."

Although, it seems like you have come to the end of your ropes with your teen and you may be considering boot camp for their troublesome behavior; you should know that there are other options.

Teens also have unreasonable expectations, especially if they are used to getting their own way. People call this 'parents spoiling their children,' by giving them everything that they ask for. If they don't get their own way, sometimes, or they realize that things are not always within their control - they get angry.

Their anger can take many forms. Some teens might hold back their anger and withdraw, while others may get disobedient, or even destructive. Some will turn to abusive behaviors such as alcoholism and drug abuse.

Various situations can bring out feelings of anger. Parents are often caught by surprise and react by either yelling or arguing back, or punishing their teen for showing their anger. This usually does not work.

Instead, parents need to see this show of anger or rage as a sign that their teen is fighting with or facing a situation that they are unable to deal with on their own, or is besieged by the demands of their daily lives.

Fortunately parents have many options to find help for their teenagers through their frustration and help them to cope with everyday pressure by:

- Asking their teen child what kind of unresolved conflict he or she is facing
- Listening to their teen child
- Helping them to focus on their feelings
- Understanding the situation from the teen's perspective

- Helping their teen child to work towards coming to a better solution
- Showing the teenager that they are loved and cared for

Unresolved issues can skyrocket to physical violence, addictions, and psychosomatic disorders.

This can ruin your teen's life by destroying relationships, interfering with effective judgment and thinking; and ruining his or her future. It is best to seek professional help for your teenager, yourself, and your family, if the situation is getting out of control.

Anger Management

Anger management for teens shows them how to analyze emotions, situations, and the issues related to why they are being opposed. Taking a few seconds to think these thoughts through; often has a good impact on their behavior.

Working with teenagers who have anger problems is often a challenge, but there are resources available to help your teen. The process of teaching teen's anger management may cause a battle between you and your teenager.

Is it really worth it to fight with your teenager or is it better to find a way to deal with both sides? I believe that your teen can control his or her anger, but it will mean that he or she has to go through a process, but once the process has been completed, anger control will be more feasible.

Your teenager needs to learn the skills to always know what to do and how to do it right when the emotions of anger come to the forefront.

The truth is it's not his or her fault that anger sometimes gets the best of them. You see the angry responses, for the most part, came as he watched the people around him display theirs from the time he was a child.

It's alright though; your teenager is not alone. There are millions of people just like your teenager who are angry and want to get their anger under control.

You should encourage your teen that it is not his or her fault that their anger is out of control, and because of this, you can provide information to your teen about how to express their anger appropriately.

Trying to cope with different situations, which are endlessly presented, is often times expressively taxing for a teenager. The strain that it causes brings many thoughts and bad feelings; especially anger. When a teenager's buttons are pushed, anger is a natural result.

Anger management for teens ensures that a teen understands self-awareness and self-control. Anger is a very powerful emotion. When it is not dealt with right, anger can cause so much destruction to the angry person and to the recipient(s). Learning to deal with these emotions at a young age will improve the teenager's adult life.

When there is evidence of anger problems in a teenager, parents should ensure that the teen gets help with it. His future can be easily changed in a negative way.

As part of the anger management program for teenagers, self-awareness is generally the primary focus initially. It means that your teen will be taught to recognize that he has the ability to evaluate the situation, which causes the anger. Encouraging him to take notice of his feelings during irritating incidents is important to his anger management.

Helping him to see the necessity of thinking during actual frustrating encounters will make a difference.

It is often difficult to maintain control of your impulses when others around us make us mad. It is even more difficult when the prices in the economy increases every year, and the legal and political system is constantly putting more demands on us every day.

Most of us deal with the stressors in life as they come our way, but some of us get out of control. Management is often the solution for treating anger; however, the person must be willing to admit their actions are causing more problems.

When a person acts out violently, verbally abusive, assault and so on it not only causes problem for the person out of control, it also causes problems for others.

Often when a person has anger issues he or she will attack others whether physically or mentally.

The angered person will often attack in a way that belittles, humiliates, harms, or threatens another life.

This person will need to learn to control his or her anger, since everyone around him or her is in a degree of danger, and sometimes more danger than others.

Anger is the inability to restrain the impulses, desires and emotions. When a person is out of contact with his emotions, it often creates a chaotic mind.

When a person is threatened, it is always good to have a degree of anger to protect. However when a person does not have control then it can lead to trouble. Anger, sadness, joy and happy are all parts of our emotions, and when we have those emotions in control we often live a productive life.

However, when we seem to a target of attack then it is more difficult for us to manage our life and anger.

For example, some children go to school and each day a bully will antagonize this child pushing him beyond his or her control.

The child may hold his feelings in for a period, but eventually he or she is going to lose control, since none of us is willing to continue allowing someone to make our lives miserable.

Unfortunately, when this child reaches his or her limits and returns the attack on the child, he then becomes the culprit and is often punished.

The bully, too, many times gets away with his behavior, and once the victim takes action he or she is often punished. The school administrator will often say why didn't you tell me what was going on?

However, the fact is the child most likely told the administrator and in my experiences, they rarely act.

Now we have two children with anger problems and more people in trouble. This is only one of the many reasons why a person cultivates anger to a degree of explosion. Each time we are angry we feel it in our body and mind.

Our body will often tense when we feel angry. If you feel this tension then it is time to step back and take control. Why am I mad? Why do I feel this way?

Asking yourself questions can help you find the answers if you search your mind hard enough. Usually after a person has developed a level of anger that is out of control, they will often strike out at persons even if there is no justifiable cause.

The person could have moved something that belonged to that person and they will react by saying something like, 'you stupid moron, why in the hell did you move my belongings?

I cannot believe how stupid you are. Why do you bother breathing?' This is only a few examples of a verbal attack issued by an angered person.

The person may attack physically by kicking, hitting, punching, spitting, or causing other types of harm to the person. It is important to get management in play if you have anger problems.

If you cannot control your emotions then one day, someone will control them for you. Anger is good if you have it under control, but when you lose control someone, someday will pay and that someone in many cases will be you as well as the trail of victims behind you.

Pressure – From Self or Peers

Teens can show anger in different ways. Some sulk. They won't talk to anyone about what's bothering them. Some pretend nothing is wrong, even though they are extremely angry inside.

Others use name-calling, teasing, yelling, or screaming to express anger. They may even get into fights. Some of these expressions can help teens deal with anger temporarily, but often, they won't make anything better.

One great coping strategy is learning self-talk. Have your teenager take 15 minutes out of each day to review their thoughts and talk them over with themselves first and then, if they feel comfortable; they can talk it over with you.

If they have a series of negative thoughts, such as 'I am a failure,' then your teen child wants to ask, 'Why do I think that I am a failure?' Have your child review all the good things that they do each day and commend themselves and when they see their mistakes; remember that everyone makes mistakes and there are probably no consequences to the mistake that was made.

If your teen son or daughter gets angry easily and wants to break things, or yell and scream; you should explain the consequences and the reality.

Tell your teenager that if they break things then they will make a mess and it needs to be cleaned up. This means they will have to do all the work to clean up the mess.

There was nothing resolved from taking those actions of breaking valuable things that may be irreplaceable. If your teenager breaks something that is not as valuable, be sure to make them pay for it. You can take the money out of their allowances or take away something that they really love; even for a while.

Explain to your teen that their actions were wasted time, energy and money. In addition, let your teenager know that yelling or screaming only upsets their heart, nerves, mind and body. This means that in the end they may have long-term medical conditions.

Now you can teach your teenager about positive anger. Taking a few short breaths might create a calming effect. It might allow your teenager to want to slow down, think for a few minutes and find a way to stress their emotions without interrupting their body, mind and health.

Teach your teen child that slowing down on a stressful day may be an easy way to handle anger caused by unnecessary stress.

Show them how to take time out for themselves and how to handle task one at a time instead of multitasking. Or if they have to multitask, teach them how to make a check list and do each task one at a time; instead of trying to do them all at one time.

Let them know that if they procrastinate; it would only make handling the task at hand more challenging and difficulty and put them into a tight spot.

It is important for your teenager to remember that they are only human and that not a superman or woman. Taking it one day at a time is often the best solution to cope with their anger.

As adults, we can teach our children how to handle bouts of anger in a more 'adult,' way by following these guidelines:

Ask yourself, "Is this worth getting angry about?" Teach your teen that sometimes it is better to ignore someone than to get into a confrontation.

If the person does not stop the behavior that's making your child angry, your child should tell the person that you are angry and why. Your child should do this without calling the person obscene names or yelling. "I don't like to be pushed around. Please stop it."

Sometimes, your child may need help in dealing with an angry person such as telling you or going to a school counselor. In this day and age, children feel intimidated doing so because their peers will cause them 'a snitch,' and their school life will never be the same.

Therefore, your teenager may not be speaking about what the cause of the anger is because of fear of being identified as a snitch. It is a lot of pressure for your teenager to endure. Other children can be cruel and terrorize your child for the rest of their time in school.

Teenagers don't fight and get the anger out of their system anymore. They go for guns and knives; bring them to school for revenge. They will go and report it to their gang friends and cause even more problems that can lead to prison.

Is it really worth getting angry over something trivial and end up in prison later? Parents need to express the reality of the situation to their teen children.

One angry moment can lead to someone getting shot. High school teenagers have access to weapons and will not hesitate in taking revenge. Parents have to warn their own children about these dangers. Peer pressure is sometimes what results in these actions.

Teenagers want to boast about their easy access to guns and knives. They want to impress their friends. So they will go to lengths to show you what they can do to you.

When I was going to school, no one would even consider taking a weapon to school. Yes, we got angry. Yes, we got into fights, but we never hurt anyone that seriously.

What is happening to this generation? Is it because of the gun laws or is it because parents are not taking matters seriously enough to ensure that their children are well informed to realize that their negative behavior will only result in serious consequences that they may not be able to handle.

Why would you be influenced by another person; when you are the only one that has to 'face the music?' This is a question that still baffles law enforcement, parents and school officials. Teenagers don't see the voice of reason when they are angry.

They may see it afterwards, but during the heat of their emotions, they only are thinking of one thing – getting even. There is so much work to be done with teenage anger. The community also has a role to play, but it first begins with the parents.

The Aggressive Teenager

For most part, teenagers are the ones most vulnerable to the damage that anger can cause since this is the stage where personalities are established and developed.

Without proper guidance from parents and teachers, teens who have anger problems will tend to carry this as they grow old, making it a deeply embedded part of what they become in the future; thus making it difficult to manage later on as well.

Before you can even broach the idea of helping teens with anger problems it is important that you know or have an idea as to how your teen displays their anger. Do they belong to the aggressive, the passives, or the schemers?

Second would be to approach the issue with caution as they might not really be up to talking about it. They will deny, clam up, or totally avoid the issue. It is important that you do not approach the problem in a dictating, demanding, scolding, or authoritative note, telling your child to straighten out his or her behavior.

Instead, show them that you understand what they are going through and offer to help if they want it. Remember that you do not want to develop resistance in any way as this will eliminate all future efforts.

It is also important that you be able to let your child know that you are not there to help eliminate anger but to help them with expressing their anger in a more constructive and less destructive way.

Also take note that your child may refuse the offer a few times before they do think about letting you help them, so patience will always be needed.

The most difficult part when trying to help teens with anger problems is getting past the walls that they have made around themselves separating them from other people.

Once you have gotten over this, take note that you will probably be given only one chance to get it right, and it is important that you succeed in order to continue the process.

Once this difficult obstacle has been passed, you will then be able to introduce anger management methods or offer further help in the form of anger management experts.

Helping teens with anger problems will not be easy, but it is something that you must not give up on, if you don't want your child to experience the devastating emotional or even physical damage that anger can cause in his or her life later on.

If you want a positive outcome you need to be flexible. If you want something from them you have to give a little. Sometimes it something simple that can get the right outcome, maybe give an extra half hour on their curfew, but tell them in that if they break the agreement that they will have consequences to pay. Lay it on the line, now they can understand.

Teens love to negotiate. Deal with them be flexible, but in this be sure you are getting what you want in the end.

Teenagers will rant and rave about not being treated fairly because you've asked them to come home at a decent time.

Parents must identify these battles for what they are. They are irrational emotional distress that will get all parties involved tangled into its web.

It can get messy and once you are in, it is, then, difficult to get out of. If you find yourself spun in this web of irrational emotional distress, you will do more harm than good by trying to prove you are the one who is right.

Parents want respect from their teenagers and don't get me wrong; parents deserve respect from their teenagers. However, this is not a problem when your child is under age 12; because your child will adore you at such young ages.

The problem comes when your child no longer has to depend totally on you and seeks their emotional independence. Because they are confused during this time of seeking independence; teens can find that they are being pulled in many different directions.

Their friends are pulling, social media networks are pulling, parents are pulling, and school is pulling. It's under this pressure that a lot of teens will react negatively to the one person that a teen can act out against without fear of retaliation--a mom or a dad.

Parents receive most of the verbal abuse. Why? Because of the old adage "You hurt the one you are with."

Parents have to learn to recognize that when their teen is hysterical about not being able to purchase a desired item such as an expensive pair of jeans, or is hysterical about not being about to hang out with their friends; not to take this personal. It is just a part of the growing up process.

The best thing a parent can do is learn to not fight their angry teen's emotions, but learn to embrace their angry teen's negative emotions. Because when it is embraced, a parent can shape and mold anger into something that no one thought possible--a smile.

Here are some quick tips:

- Learn to negotiate
- Don't get angry

- Get into your teen's world by trying to learn their language, their music and their likes and dislikes.
- Give your teenager some space.
- Remember that you were once a teenager so be patient and reasonable.
- Be the parent. You are not your teenager's friend. There is a time and place for that and you don't want to confuse your child. You want your child to know and accept certain boundaries from a young age.
- Let your child know that even though you are a parent, you make mistakes too

These days, teenage stress and aggression can become a serious problem. Life for teens today just isn't as simple as when parents went through it.

Our kids are bombarded with challenges that we never had. It is important to learn what you can do to help your teen through this challenging and formative time.

Never before has so much information been available from so many sources. It used to be that if a teen had a tough day at school or a fight with a friend; they could at least seek the safety of home.

Now, thanks to technology, there is no escape. Things like texting, email and instant messages can keep constant stress and pressure on your child. Many teens do not know how to deal with this and act out aggressively towards friends, siblings and parents.

It is important to monitor your teen's mood and behavior at several key points in the day to find the root cause of stress and aggression. Almost like a daily diagnostic checklist.

Happy in the morning...check.

Happy after school...check.

Moody after online chat with friends...source discovered!

Once a source of stress is discovered, it is important to take action immediately. If a round of texting has created the problem, it is not likely that your teen will text their way out of it.

This does not mean you simply take the cell phone away from your teen and solve the problem.

This will probably just make things worse. The best approach is to talk to your child and give them the opportunity to work the problem out with you. Yes, I know it is not that easy talking to an angry teen, but it will get easier for both of you if you continue to have an open dialogue.

Other teenage stress factors can include an overbooked schedule.

It is great to have your teen involved in sports and school events, but too many planned activities can be the cause of teen stress.

It is important to make wise decisions with your teen about how they will spend their time and what groups and activities are worth pursuing.

Let your teenagers decide how much workload they can manage. You don't want to be the one to push things on them.

Another key factor in the mood of you teen is sleep. What is really happening when they head off to bed? If they are not sleeping enough you may need to address the distractions in their room.

Things like televisions, computers, video games and cell phones can cause a teen to stay up for hours.

Lack of sleep could contribute to teenage stress and aggression. In addition, with a television in a teen's room, it is hard for parents to monitor what they are watching.

There is a lot of aggression on television that your teenager can emulate in their own daily lives. So, as parents, we need to take stock of what our teenager is doing and put a lid on it.

Of course, this will make them angry, but you can have some kind of compromise and work matters out with your teenager. However, always explain why you are doing this.

When I was growing up, my parents just did whatever they wanted. Their rule was the final say. I did not get to make choices and they did not explain why they were taking certain actions.

A teenager is an individual; growing into adulthood and I personally think that we should treat them with respect and not be as 'backward,' as our parents were.

Times have change and if you want a peaceful home, you better change the way you raise your own children.

Don't take note of everything that your parents did to you. It won't work. It will only make your life more miserable.

We all know that the teen years are not easy and will include some mood swings and tense times. When it goes beyond occasional behavioral problems you will need to act. Changing behavior is best done early on.

It will be more difficult to break the patterns of stress and anger the longer you wait.

Depending on the level of anger and aggression you may need to seek the help of an anger management counselor.

This can be a difficult but it is important to you help before the aggression leads to serious problems.

Anger from a Divorce or Separation

Teenagers are at a unique crossroads in life: not quite grown up, but no longer young children. Teens deal with emotional issues much differently than either younger kids or adults, and therefore a divorce affects a teenager differently as well.

A teenager may exhibit a variety of reactions to news of divorce, including anger, depression, feelings of guilt, taking sides, outbursts, or even refusing to speak about the event at all.

By understanding how teenagers may be deal with their emotions, you can help your own teen through this difficult time.

Divorce and separation was looked upon with disdain in past years, but today, it has become quite easy for parents to split up.

Some of the divorce cases are so horrific that it damages the children in an almost irreparable way. Many mothers and fathers are raising their children singlehandedly.

Couples that make the decision to separate or divorce usually have their own issues to deal with, but in most instances, they overlook the interests of their children who are at a greater loss during this delicate change in their family life.

For both genders; male and female, it is very essential for teenagers to have an ongoing connection with both the parents as each has a role to play in their lives to guide them to fully develop their personality without any negative character traits.

Most children are not able to express the distress that they feel when both parents are no longer speaking.

This results in behavioral problems that can be linked with the absence of a parent initially. Psychological evaluation of such children always reveals the fact that the teen's problems are related to the missing interaction with the other parent.

When a divorce takes place, usually the parents are too busy to take notice of any emotional change in the teenager who is being equally affected by this recent change.

Changes are different for various age groups and personalities, but the most common change for all ages is "Depression and Anger," which they show in different ways such as:

- Failing grades in school
- Losing their appetite
- Lack of interest in sports and other activities
- Spending more time away from home with other teenager friends

- Aggressive behavior
- Squabble with other siblings
- Sleep disorders
- Unexpected health issues
- Getting in trouble in school

A parent should always think of the well being of their children. The ideal situation would be avoiding the separation or the divorce, but we don't live in a perfect world. If this is not possible, then both parents should find a way to continue the ongoing interaction with the children; despite their differences.

It is okay for your teenager to be angry. Suddenly, routines are changed and life is now completely different in a one-parent household.

Anger is an extension of sadness and fear-your teen may be scared about the future and sad about the present situation.

Consider seeking outside emotional support for your teen so that he or she may vent anger in a productive and healthy environment.

In certain cases, when this is not possible, the parent who has custody of the children has to be more involved to reduce their children's stress.

Most importantly, a teenager should never be blamed for the situation that led to the separation between the parents, nor should the absent parent be blamed unnecessarily for the decision as it will be unfair to both parties.

In order to reduce teenage stress about the separation or the divorce, you have to understand that you are not the only one who has gone through such traumatic situation.

The child feels a greater loss. Parents may find another partner, but a child feels that he or she will never be able to replace the biological parent who is absent from the home.

Your teen may decide to blame you or your ex-spouse as the reason for the divorce. It can be difficult to deal with this situation, especially if the teen has blamed you.

Try talking with both your teen and your ex-spouse about the situation, and understand that taking sides is just another way of dealing with fear and anger.

Sometimes teenagers seem to be fine with the divorce and do not talk about the situation with either you or your ex-spouse. Although your teen may be dealing with the divorce in a healthy way, make sure that your teen is not internalizing all emotions.

He or she may want or need to speak to someone, but may be uncomfortable talking to you or your ex-spouse. Encourage dialogue between your teen and his or her friends or a trusted adult.

Some teens overcompensate for their parent's decision. They overcompensate by getting better grades, working harder at home, participating in more afterschool programs and getting more recognition in the process.

They may feel guilty about the divorce and think that if they just get their grades up or if they become "better sons/daughters", their parents would stay together.

Teens who believe that their efforts would make their family and home life more desirable to their parents often end up extremely disappointed when their parents push through with the divorce. This can initiate the anger, which can get out of control.

You can reduce their stress by adopting a few simple remedies:

- Spend more time and give extra affection to your children with frequent hugs and kisses.
- Talk to them about the issues relative to their age and make them understand it in the simplest terms.
- Give them extra attention and this will also help both of you through the initial phase.

Let the children stay in contact with the other parent and exchange information with your ex spouse so that you both know how the children

are feeling about it and how the family is going to cope with things in the long run.
Many teens already go through periods of mood swings.

Add divorce to the equation and you have a more volatile teenager on your hands. Teens that are having a hard time accepting or dealing with their parents' divorce often become extremely defiant; they act out, lash out in anger at their parents, or engage in dangerous activities. This is when parents have to seek professional help for the entire family unit.

Sometimes, the efforts of well-meaning parents are not enough to help teens deal with the aftermath of divorce.

It would help to keep your eyes open for these effects and similar symptoms in order to address the issue the soonest time possible and in the most effective and healthy way.

The Rebellious Teenager

Many teens today are like a ship without a rudder - floating along aimlessly through life, pounded by their ever-changing emotions. Many of them do not feel as if they were born to fulfill a purpose. Some doubt that anyone really loves them at all!

Peer pressure in combination with an intense desire to be loved and accepted, can lead many teens down the wrong path in life.

Finding their "worth" in the wrong group of friends often comes from a fear of rejection and the frightening prospect that they will be labeled as "not good enough" by those around them that they want to please.

Anger is a great cover for such insecurities, or so they believe. The anger that teenagers show is sometimes due to fear. This fear is magnified by their lack of problem solving abilities.

Of course, our society tends to use more socially acceptable titles for fear (we don't want to think of ourselves as "afraid" - that sounds too wimpy).

These titles include:

- Anxiety
- Insecurity
- Worry
- Uncertainty
- Distrust

- Depression
- Sadness

If you stop and think about it for a few minutes, you are likely to pinpoint some of these areas of struggle in a teen that you know and love.

Helping teens to learn and embrace these problem-solving abilities can lessen anger and promote a new level of understanding and responsibility.

There is much we can do to help prepare them for the day when they will be on their own. The world doesn't have to be such a scary place - there are tools to help prepare teens for a brighter future. It's up to us as adults to arm our teens with these tools.

When a teenager does not understand the deep seated reasons for their bad attitude, they will tend to become rebellious.

Sometimes, this is only a way for them to seek the attention of the people closest to them; including their parents. Often, anger is a cover, or mask, for some other underlying emotion.

Teens may be rebellious for a variety of reasons, and it may display in numerous behaviors including:

- Chronic disrespect
- Bad Attitude
- Intentional breaking of rules

- Lying
- Stealing
- Bullying behavior
- Verbal or physical aggression

Teen rebellion is certainly not limited to boys, either. Teen girls can be just as challenging as their male counterparts at times.

So many parents of young children joke about "the rebellious years" in a teenager's life, saying they're getting ready for the talking back or the "regular" teenage problems.

They sometimes reminisce about their own teen years, making comments like, "I know what I was doing or thinking at that age and it wasn't good!" For many parents of teenagers, however, rebellion is a regular occurrence in their lives and it affects the entire family dynamic.

This vicious circle often begins with the teen acting out and the parents reacting, which usually prompts the teen to react even more.

Pretty soon the situation has escalated and even if the younger siblings aren't directly involved, they witness the scenes and feel the tension in the home.

Sometimes the rebellion is simply the teen trying to discover him or herself. They might blame their parents for being too strict and might start dressing differently just to get a reaction for not fitting into the family "mold."

Or maybe their grades might slip because they're tired of the pressure to always perform well. This type of rebellion is usually just a phase that diminishes with time and maturity.

"Rebelling" is almost synonymous with "teenagers" but if parents stay connected with their teen and show support and willingness to communicate, the rebelling can often be less stressful.

Just remember that your teen is trying to find his or her way in the world and sometimes those are tough lessons to learn.

Raising a rebellious teenager is especially difficult and the suggestions in this article will help to make dealing with your rebellious teenager just a little bit easier.

Here are some reminder tips if you find your teen is starting to rebel against you. Please remember that there are many different courses of action and not one solution will work for everyone.

It's vitally important to assess your own child's behavior without comparing to other teen friends or family members.

Remember that you are the parent, not the friend. Parents are responsible for setting limits and boundaries and sometimes this role is muddied in younger childhood.

Do not be afraid to set limits, enforce house rules, and to voice your expectations. Don't expect your teenaged child to be a mind reader...have a conversation or write down the rules so everybody is on the same page.

Compromising is not giving in. If your child rebels against your rules and thinks you're too strict, why not try to compromise with him/her?

This isn't to say, "OK, do it your way," but rather gives your child a change to use his or her thinking skills to come up with a different solution. This give and take is an important life lesson to be utilized in their adult years.

It's OK to dislike your teen's behavior and it's OK to tell them so. Believe it or not, this stranger in your house is the same little kid you used to push on the swing.

However, be sure to differentiate between loving the child and disliking the child's behavior. Good kids often do bad things or make big mistakes and showing forgiveness and support is better than giving up on them.

Seek out medical help if you fear for your child's safety. There are certain situations that are simply out of a parent's control and require the help of professionals.

Sometimes parents live in denial or a much idealized world, thinking they can solve the child's every problem.

Big problems rarely disappear on their own so don't be ashamed of asking your doctor or school counselor for help, especially if the child's behavior makes you fear for someone's safety. Remember your own teen years.

If you felt stressed and rebelled as a teen, think about what would have helped you through that time?

Tell your teen that you went through this period as well and some of the hard lessons you learned. Also remember that being a teen now is much more difficult than in years past.

Children are growing up faster and having adult experiences much younger, thanks in part to the internet, social media, and peer pressure.

Listen to your teen. Yes, you might be thinking why your teenager would open up to you in the midst of rebelling but teens are unpredictable.

An incident at school or with a friend might spur the need to ask questions and parents need to be receptive to this opportunity.

Teens often have to build up strength to start serious conversations and telling them to "Wait until after dinner," most likely will shut them down for good.

Decide what the rules are in your family, and let your family members become aware of it at an early age.

If you have to write them down and post them in a visible area such as the kitchen, then by all means do so. Children, inherently, want to have boundaries.

They want to know what you expect of them. Some will push the limit, but for the most part, once they understand your expectations as parents, it will be easier to reason with your teenager. Some cases are more difficult and this is when you would need outside help.

Conclusion

Your teenager needs you more than he or she thinks. However, they won't act that way. They will act as if they are already adults and expect to be treated that way; even though, they still live under your roof, don't have a job and cannot exist on their own.

You may not always agree with your teenager, but while you listen to their gripe; wait until they get done telling you what is on their mind, and then you can tell them the way it should be. One big factor I believe in parent-teenager relationships is not getting angry.

This is a reaction they expect us to have and when we don't show anger; it can lead to a more reasonable solutions.

Remember, if you lose your temper, then this is what you are teaching them to do. Some families seem to go through the teen years with little or no struggle.

Many others find these years one of the most challenging and, at times, maddening stages of family life.

One of the areas that seem to be most difficult for them has to do with trust. Families sometimes get stuck because the parents see trust as an issue in the teenager years.

The teenager will lie, break curfews, experiment with drugs or does something that's damaging to trust. The parents feel they have lost all trust in their teen. When the parent speaks out, the teenager will then get angry and the angry builds.

Many parents resort to just coping with a troubled teenager - ignore him or her and the problem will go away. But it doesn't! In reality this kind of behavior doesn't simply go away. More often than not, it just gets worse.

One of life's most stressful times often occurs during that exasperating period known as the teen age - it is often 7 years of pure hell. And there you are, frustrated and clueless as to how to eradicate this bizarre behavior.

At times you must wish for some magic potion that would suddenly turn them into adults. Well the solution doesn't reside in a bottle of pills, but there is hope and I'll get into that in a moment.

If you are experiencing disrespect, you probably have seen it appear in many forms. What is needed is to discover the causes (yes there are probably multiple causes) of this behavior.

No doubt you wonder whatever happened to your once lovable child. How did your child become so irritable, seemingly uncontrollable alien?

Experts tell us that with some teens, the problems are rooted in some type of identity crisis. Your child didn't become this possessed creature overnight.

Is the problem an "identity crisis?" Is your teenager obsessed with trying to figure out just who he or she really is? Is the child wondering what the future holds? "What's to become of me?"

Many times the child is feeling resentment for the life he or she has lived up to that point and is struggling to escape it. Well, we can't change the past but we as parents can paint a picture of a brighter future.

What the child needs most when life's pressures seem unbearable is your love and compassion. And granted...that's a tough order when the child is screaming at you.

Yes, in seven years, your teenager will be an adult, but their teenage years seem like it will last a lifetime.

A good parent wants the best for the child - get good grades in school, get into a good college and start a healthy, productive life - even at the risk of seeming over-protective.

But most rebellious teens really don't give a damn about the future...they want to feel good NOW!

Along the way you must have established certain ground rules. You and I know how important this is for natural growth among us human beings.

However, have you considered allowing the child to have a say when rules are put down? Giving the child more say in how the family operates will often cool some of the rebelliousness.

Of course this has to be tempered with good judgment. When misbehavior occurs - point it out while being calm and understanding. And of course yelling to make a point only increases the tension between you.

Avoid being argumentative at all costs. Neither side ever wins an argument. Give the child support and understanding.

Empower your teenage child by assigning certain simple responsibilities.

Every action taken by an individual has consequences - including teenage behavior. These consequences may be good or bad. The idea is to instill in the child the need to take a moment to think about the possible outcome of his or her actions.

Open the lines of communications with your teenager. If it has fallen victim to current practice, then re-establish the family dinner.

Face to face conversation can soothe the anger and resentment. Give your teenager a measure of respect. You expect it from him or her. Be generous and dole it out whenever they do something worth praising.

If you are a step parent like me and dealing with teenagers, it is an entirely different situation. In fact, it might be even more difficult than if you were the biological parent. You have to tread very carefully with teenagers if you are a step parent.
Step-parents often experience rejection and anger from the step-child in the teenage years. After giving so much loving care over the years, it can be more than a parent can bear when the child seemingly turns against them in the teen years.

It doesn't matter that you have been a loving parent to the child for many years. He or she still longs for the missing parent, or the perception of the way things used to be.

The teen longs for the family to look like other families, or to have both parents together. He or she may even incorrectly believe that their life would be happy and free of problems if things hadn't changed.

And here's the kicker, every time the teen sees you; he or she is reminded of what he or she no longer has and truly wants down deep – both biological parents under one roof.

In trying to "fix" the attitudes and behavior of a wayward step-child, I often see parents try to bribe the child into better behavior or mood by providing things that the child may want; by letting them do whatever they want, or by looking the other way when they step out of line.

However, for the parent, such behavior is out of line and will ultimately lead to deeper issues for the child and the parent.

The goal for any parent; step-parent or not, is simply this: to guide a child into being a productive member of society, to develop social and civil behavior and to teach the child to survive and thrive in the world.

Those standards are not always supported by a parent whose primary goal is to keep their children happy all the time.

The best approach to take is to maintain your proper parental role, recognizing what you can and cannot change for your teenager.

For instance, you can't change the feelings of loss, or the past decisions that affect the teen today. You can't change the facts of her current circumstances.

You can't change what may have happened outside of the realm of your control.

It makes no sense to demand a step-child to stop feeling the way he or she does or to constantly emphasize all you have done for the teenager. Instead, if things are becoming difficult, find a good counselor to help the teen work through the loss.

Eventually that will change the way he or she thinks and behaves. I'm not saying it will be easy for either parents or step parents, but taking this approach allows you to continue to deal with behavioral issues by enforcing rules and applying consequences, while a counselor deals with the emotional issues.

Since every child is unique and different; the methods of anger management may rely on personalized attention.

Speaking to the child extensively is what may provide the information you need as a parent or counselor to dig deep into the cause of the teen's behavior.

Combined with therapy, counseling and firm, but flexible parenting, teenagers can enjoy the years that seem so challenging to them.

Parents should have hope and remember that you are not alone. We all went through those formative years and it was not easy for us or for our parents.

Don't worry about those years if you are not there yet. When it comes, you will deal with each child one-on-one. Some teenagers don't have the kind of volatile teen years as others do, so worrying about it now is only going to cause unnecessary anxiety and stress.

However, learn as much as you can about teenagers today because they are very different from the years that you and I spent as teenagers. Technology advancement has created a 'monster,' which we have to learn how to deal with.

If we don't learn about computers, twitter, Facebook; how teenagers communicate with each other and how the school system is run, we will never know how to deal with our teenagers.

I know for a fact that being flexible, listening to your child and allow your child to be the unique individual that he or she was created to be will set the stage for a loving and happy relationships. All the best to you!

Printed in the USA
CPSIA information can be obtained
at www.ICGtesting.com
LVHW010235281024
794972LV00001B/74